Prayers for the Broken-Hearted

Debbie Kay

Copyright © 2012 Hope for the Broken-Hearted

Cover design by Jeff Little

Book design by Jeff Little

Enhanced Text read by Debbie Kay

Other enhanced audio read by Sandy Sooter

All rights reserved.

No part of this book may be reproduced in any form or by any electronic or mechanical means including information storage and retrieval systems, without permission in writing from the author. The only exception is by a reviewer, who may quote short excerpts in a review.

Printed in the United States of America

First Printing: November 2012

ISBN-10: 0988580438

ISBN-13: 978-0-9885804-3-5

Dedication

This book is dedicated to...

My Lord and Savior, Jesus Christ -
You are my Healer, Provider, and my Source of Hope...

And to my son, Ryan -
You are my greatest gift from God and the joy of my life. I love you!!

Acknowledgments

There are so many people that I love, who have supported me and encouraged me through the years and I would like to mention everyone by name because you are dear to my heart. But to do so, would make the acknowledgements in this book, longer than this book itself. So, I want to acknowledge those who have played a major part in our lives during the trials that led up to the creation of my ministry and this book.

My Mom and Dad… I have been blessed more than I deserve to have you as my parents. Thank you for the many ways you have encouraged and supported me in my life. You have had such an influence on my life, by teaching me about Jesus when I was young. You showed me by your example, how to be a compassionate person and how to love my child with a sacrificial love. Ryan and I both know our lives would be very different if we had not had your help the last eight years. We are more grateful than you will ever know. I love you both.

Mavis Johnson, Dr. Lucretia Reed, Dr. Sharon Teruya, and Fred Gant, you were our life lines that kept us tethered to this world in our darkest days. I will always be forever grateful to you. You were the tangible hands and feet of Jesus to Ryan and me. You helped us pick up the shattered pieces of our broken hearts and put them back together again and there are not words enough to say what a difference you have made in our lives. From the bottom of my heart, "Thank you."

My grandmothers, Gladys Neal and Bonnie Brandenburg… Thank you for the many ways that you have blessed our lives and shown your love… You are loved more than you'll ever know.

Betty and Kenny Neal and Bonnie and Mike Dino… You have been so supportive of me my whole life. Your support and encouragement, especially the last eight years, has humbled me and blessed me. I love you all so very much!

Josh Martinez… You were there for us in ways that no one else was. You have a special place in my heart forever, because of your loving kindness, support and acts of compassion. You are so loved and forever you are the son of my heart.

Beth Brandenburg… Thanks for being a listening ear whenever I needed it. You, Mark, Caprice and Troy have stood by us and shown your love and support in so many tangible ways. We both love you. We are grateful to you and for you.

Debbie Kelly… What an incredible gift and blessing you have been in my life. I pray the Lord blesses you tenfold for your generous, compassionate heart. I love you, my dear friend.

Foreword

It was a terribly exhausting time… I didn't want to pray; I felt God was absent, on a long vacation, or handling things around the world that appeared much bigger than what was happening in my small world. However, my small world was crashing, which was a very huge problem. I had tried every spiritual discipline I could think of; each time I grew more tired and more frustrated… Where was God as my small, but only, world was falling to pieces? Then one afternoon, I first began to understand prayer. I said to the Lord,

"God, I don't think you are listening or really caring about what is happening in my life; the pain is relentless, things are going from bad to worse, and telling you about it makes me angry because I feel forgotten. And because I can't think of another thing to try, may I just lay my head down and rest… not read another devotional or try a new 3 or 4-step structure to 'making' prayer work?"

I kid you not, there wasn't some angry thrash from heaven, some lightning or ethereal, frightening occurrence… I laid my head down and a peace filled my heart that had not been there before. It was as if the Lord was longing for me to come to the end of 'life' that day and let Him provide what was needed. How different that is from what most of us consider to be prayer.

For most of us, prayer is often a perplexing subject. Questions quickly surface in a scattered sort of way... What do I say; who am I really talking to; does it matter; isn't prayer for holiday meals and funerals; and don't people - like Monks, clergy, or those very spiritual - have more effective prayers than I do? We think of prayer as a saintly, sacred, somewhat mystical sort of behavior... It sounds so clinical, doesn't it? However, prayer is wonderfully simple... but our worries, questions, assumptions, and expectations can complicate things. So often, prayer feels like another "to do" thing on that ever-growing list that we toss the 'discipline' of actually doing it because one more demanding duty pushes us over the edge.

If you have ever had any of those thoughts or discomforts, this book on prayer will revolutionize your life because prayer is about a relationship... and in healthy relationships, there is time to speak and times of quietness, moments of rest and struggle, and – trust me on this – frustration, confusion, and consideration that comes along when we are in a relationship with someone. In prayer, our relationship is with Jesus Christ. If you don't know Jesus, then prayer makes little sense; however, being in relationship with Christ is very simple. It begins by saying:

"Lord God, I believe you are listening to me. I am broken and in need of help... of a Savior... Who will walk with me and comfort me, and create in me a new heart... that is filled with hope and peace because You promise to never leave me or forsake me. So now, I ask that You come into my heart, that You take up residence in my life, and that You show me what it's like to know You, trust You, and talk with You for the rest of my life. Amen."

"<u>*Prayers for the Broken-Hearted*</u>" is a refreshing, authentic, synergistic offering to any person longing for companionship and comfort. The pictures of nature are visual reminders of how great our Creator is; the words are simple, deep, and full of need as well as profound peace and promises of comfort and hope. Much of prayer includes listening and quietness. In fact, one writer said, "Do not be afraid of silence in your prayer time. It may be that you are meant to listen, not to speak. So wait before the Lord. Wait in silence." (Amy Carmichael) Chuck Swindoll said, "In solitude, struggles occur that no one else knows about... God, who probes our deepest thoughts during protracted segments of solitude, opens our eyes to things that need attention."

My friend, if you have ever felt lonely, weak, in pain or need, financially drained, misunderstood, betrayed, empty, longing for a change in perspective, under the veil of darkness, forgotten, without hope, depressed, or in need of comfort, those are the subjects of prayer you bring to Jesus Christ. First, He endured every experience of suffering; so He understands you. Next, He spoke to His Father when the suffering did not end. Prayer doesn't mean our suffering will end; it means we have placed our trust in Christ who promises to love without condition, to be faithful to every promise He's given to us in His Word, to hear us at all times… He never sleeps or slumbers. But we must also remember, prayer is a transforming process in our souls. There is not always healing, instant relief, incessant joy; nor is God our grand 'bellhop' who answers our every call. Pride would have us believe that. Prayer is about seeing every part of God, telling Him about every part of you, and then watching Him work in your broken circumstances and changing our perspective along the way.

My prayer for you today comes from the prayer of Paul the Apostle at the beginning of his letter to the Ephesians. He includes these words: *"I keep asking that the God of our Lord Jesus Christ, the glorious Father, may give you the Spirit of wisdom and revelation, so that you may know him better. I pray that the eyes of your heart may be enlightened in order that you may know the hope to which he has called you, the riches of his glorious inheritance in his holy people, and his incomparably great power for us who believe. That power is the same as the mighty strength he exerted when he raised Christ from the dead and seated him at his right hand in the heavenly realms, far above all rule and authority, power and dominion, and every name that is invoked, not only in the present age but also in the one to come. (Ch 1:18-21)*

I encourage you to sit with this work, to allow these prayers to speak to and through your soul. May they reveal the true nature of God and the vast condition of our need as human beings. Perhaps you may even want to lay your head down and rest as I did that afternoon. Allow the prayers to speak for you… In silence, you will find Jesus Christ, as you have never known Him before.

Colleen Swindoll Thompson

Introduction

My ministry, "Hope for the Broken-Hearted," came out of personal experiences I have been through. These experiences gave me a strong desire to help others to deal with their grief. But what really brought this ministry to life, was answered prayer. What I prayed to the Lord was based on the prayer of Jabez. My prayer was, "Bless me, Lord, so I can bless others and expand my territory." I should tell you, that while I was praying this, I was bedridden. I was dealing with health problems and multiple surgeries that left me unable to do much of anything for over two years. It really was a prayer of faith. Our God honors a sincere, heartfelt prayer. God has answered that humble prayer, in ways that have made it abundantly clear that He, alone, was the one who answered. No one can take credit but Him.

Around the time that I started praying this prayer, my nephew put an album that I had recorded twenty years earlier up on MySpace. I really didn't think anything would come of it. I thanked him for his loving support and thought that would be the end of it. Several months later, I received requests to play my songs from several radio stations in different countries. To say the least, I was amazed and shocked. I also received requests to perform at a local Christian venue. I politely declined saying I didn't perform or sing any longer. I also explained that I was laid up in bed. When I received requests again several months later, I knew this was no fluke, this was a "God thing." This sort of thing just doesn't happen with twenty year old music! Within a few weeks, my music was playing on the radio and I was doing a live, twenty-minute radio interview with a station in Scotland. I shared my testimony of how God had answered my prayer that led up to the interview. One of my songs was put up against two others, for callers to vote on for their favorite. Mine was the winner... Only God can do that! A couple of months later, I did my first concert in twenty years. We have an amazing God who is full of surprises and He does hear our prayers. If I was to share with you all that has happened since then... all of my story... well, that would take a whole book itself. I have no doubt that book will come one day! For now, the thing I wish to share is what led to this book.

As part of my ministry, I started a page on Facebook. I post scriptures, words of encouragement and prayers. On February 16, 2012 I had about 1200 fans and reached about two hundred people a week. Well, God decided to answer the rest of my prayer to expand my territory. All of a sudden, people started flocking to my page out of the blue. At one point, they were coming at the rate of 1,000 an hour. At the end of two weeks, I had 80,000 fans. Today, seven months later, my page has over 170,000 fans and is reaching on average 9.5 to 10.5 million unique people per week. I ended up starting three support groups on Facebook to help all of these people that were coming to my page. Between the three groups at this writing, we have over 2500 people. My ministry now shares a message of hope, weekly, in all 50 states and at last count, 86 countries. That, my friends, shows the power of prayer!

In February, when all of these people started coming to the page there were so many people in need and wanting prayer. I couldn't possibly pray, individually, for each one, so I posted some prayers that addressed groups of requests in an all-inclusive way. I did this several days in a row. When I didn't post one on the fourth day, I started getting messages asking where the daily prayer was. So, in response, I now write a daily prayer. They have touched many hearts and lives and I see such a need for prayer, world-wide. One of the things I heard over and over again was "you know just what to pray for." I recently read a wonderful book by Charles Stanley on prayer. In it, he stated that part of the reason God allows us to go through trials is so we will know what to pray for others. Because I have been through many trials and much adversity, I do understand so much of what people write and share with me. I do know what to pray for on behalf of the hurting, because of all that I have been through. I didn't realize - that was why my prayers were connecting with so many until I read that passage from Dr. Stanley. God wastes nothing in our lives, friends! What the enemy meant for harm, God will use for good.

About the time that I felt God urging me to write a book of prayers, I started receiving inquiries from fans wondering if I had written any books with prayers. So, this book is a product of God's leading and the requests of those who read my daily prayers.

I pray that you will also be blessed by these prayers. I pray they will give you strength. I have received countless praise reports from people that have prayed the daily prayers with us. I want to encourage you. There is hope. There is healing. God is with you in your times of need. He promises that He is near to the broken-hearted and that He will bind up their wounds. He hears your cries. He sees your tears. He hears your prayers.

Blessings, hugs and love to you,
Debbie Kay

Day 1

Dear Lord, we come before You and lift all that are dealing with broken hearts. We pray for those whose hearts feel shattered and beyond repair. What I've come to know, Lord, is it's possible to live through pain we never thought imaginable. We pray that You would infuse Your hope into those who are praying with us now, Lord… For those who feel lonely and cut off from love… For those who feel like they don't even want their hearts to be revived because they don't want to be vulnerable to pain again. Please, fill them with Your love and Your hope and restore the shattered pieces of their hearts and lives, Lord.

We pray for the hearts that are weary and sad and beat up by the things of the world. Lord, You promise to bind our wounds. You promise to re-work us like a potter works with clay. So, Lord we are asking that as You heal broken hearts, You would replace them with:

A heart that remembers all the times You've been faithful…

A forgiving heart for what has hurt us…

A grateful heart for our blessings…

A brave heart to face all that is before us…

An open heart to all that You bring into our lives…

A trusting heart that is unafraid to move forward…

A loving heart that puts You before all others…

And a willing heart to say "Yes" to whatever You will for us…

Replenish our hearts today, Lord. Orient it towards You. Allow our hearts to heal… Allow our hearts to feel… Allow us to act and move forward and renew our passion for You. Give us strength for the day and hope for tomorrow. Help us to trust You and know You like never before. Help us to keep our eyes and heart focused on You this day. In Jesus' name we pray, Amen.

Day 2

Dear Heavenly Father, we come asking that You shine a light in the dark places in our hearts. Lord, our lives are so complicated with many layers of hurts, scars and wounds. We peel off one layer and then we find another layer of pain or heartache or anger that we didn't realize was there… Or it was forgotten… Or perhaps we tried to pretend it isn't there.

Lord, we want to live in the fullness that comes from being Your child. Help us not to bury things away because we are afraid to face them. Help us not to hide things in shame or guilt. You see all… You know all about us and You love us unconditionally… Just as we are. If You can accept us, help us not worry about others accepting us, Lord. Help us to bring the secret, dark, things into the light so we can deal with them once and for all. Help us to bury the skeletons hiding in our closets so we can find Your peace. Lord, we pray for peaceful sleep for those who are having trouble, for whatever reason. We know so many deal with sleep deprivation and it makes us more emotional. It makes us more sensitive… It makes it more difficult to heal and to tolerate stress. So, we ask for healing in this area, Lord.

We ask for healing for those who are feeling nervous and stressed as they are going through their dark times. We pray that You'd help them to find peace in the storms. We pray, Lord, that You'd teach them how to relax. We ask that You'd calm upset stomachs and all the nervous disorders. We ask for healing for panic attacks and PTSD and anxiety disorders and depression. Lord, we speak forth healing in Jesus' name and we trust and believe according to Your will, that You are already working in each body, even as we are praying.

Lord, we see this picture of this amazing, serene, calm place You've made on this earth and we ask that when we start to feel overwhelmed, that we would get a mental picture of this place. We ask that You would help everyone's hearts and bodies to heal so they may feel as peaceful and calm as this picture. We know we can do all things through You, Lord, so we ask for Your help to find Your supernatural peace that passes all understanding.

Thank You, Lord, for hearing our prayers. We look forward with excited anticipation for the work that You are going to do in each of us. In Jesus' name, Amen.

Day 3

Dear Lord, so many are having hard days. Loved ones need miracles... People are plagued with doubts, fears and confusion. Lord, we thank You that You are in the midst of it all.

Thank You, that there is nowhere we can go that You are not already there. Thank You, that You are in the hospital rooms with those who are clinging to life. Thank You, that You are with those who are helplessly watching their children and loved ones make choices that they know are wrong, yet are powerless to do anything about. Thank You, that You are beside those in the pit of depression and struggle. Thank You, that You are with those in financial crisis and You are walking beside those whom we love, who don't know You yet. You are just waiting for them to call Your name so You can swoop in and make Your presence known.

Lord, thank You, that no eye has seen, nor ear heard, the things that await those who love You. Thank You, that Your hand is never shortened that it cannot reach us. Thank You, that You hear the righteous cry and You are near the crushed in spirit.

Thank You, Lord, for Your peace that passes all understanding. Thank You so much, that You gave us Your only Son, so if we believe, we will not perish. Thank You, that You gave a good plan for each of us... A plan to give us a hope and a future. Thank You, that there is a day coming when there will be no more death, fear, crying, illness or sorrow. Thank You, that You forgive us our sins and that Your grace and mercy are without bounds and Your love for us is infinite. Thank You, that one day we will be in Your presence and never feel lonely, empty, unworthy or ashamed again. Thank You, Lord, for Your Word that has endured... Thank You, that Your promises are true and that they are for each of us and for every generation.

Lord, sometimes when life is hard, the best thing we can do is to dwell on all the things we have to be grateful and thankful for. For those facing adversity or loss, may these words remind them of all You have graciously given... May these words remind them that You are as close as a breath away... May they be reminded that Jesus Himself is sitting beside them, interceding on their behalf. May they be reminded that their battles are already won and the enemy defeated.

We love You, Lord, and we thank You for Who You are and for all You've done in our lives. We bless You and praise You that You know the needs before they are spoken and You have already gone before us and made a way with abundant provision. With humble gratitude we say thank You, Lord... Thank You, Jesus. Amen.

Day 4

Dear Lord, we gather together once again, strangers geographically, yet united together in one voice because of You. Lord, You are surely in our midst the same as if we were sitting in the same room. We ask that You would fill our hearts with Your love, Your peace and Your compassion. Lord, there may be brokenness in this life, but in that brokenness we find more of You. Lord, fill the broken, empty places in our hearts, minds and lives with more of Yourself. Lord, even though there is loss, we can still have the fullness of joy because Jesus is in our hearts... It's a joy that the world cannot take away. Let my brothers and sisters know that joy, Lord... The joy that comes from knowing that no matter what this world takes away from us, we have You... And if that is all we have, it is more than enough.

Lord, thank You, that You suffered everything while You were here... Loneliness, doing without the comforts of life, rejection, anxiety, abuse, grief and loss... All so we can say that we have a Savior that understands our pain. Lord, help us to grow in our faith so that we can learn to see that suffering draws us into fellowship with You in ways we cannot know in the good times.

Lord, I pray for peace through the storms, strength for the day, love and fellowship with others so they don't feel alone. I pray for knowledge of Your Word to increase, even memorizing and calling Scriptures to mind in times of distress... Using it as the primary weapon against the enemy's lies. Inspire us to learn about and use the spiritual armor You provide us, found in Ephesians 6, that we may be able to withstand any weapon fashioned against us to defeat us. Lord, this world is not our home... We are just passing through... And life can be hard, we can grow weary, but we soldier on, not by ourselves, but with You by our side and with an invisible host standing beside us, fighting unseen enemies that would love to see us defeated.

You have not left us empty-handed... You provide a way of escape for everything we face. Bind the enemy and protect each one. Put a hedge of protection around them and their families. Meet their every need, Lord... Give them boldness and confidence along with Your power so they can face all that is before them. Lord, I know You want to bring them to a place in their spiritual lives to which they've never been before... May they be fearless like David was before Goliath, as Daniel was in the lions' den, as Joshua was in battle... All of these men of faith faced seemingly impossible odds, but they all had You in their corner and because of that, they could not lose. It's the same for each of Your children here... May they feel empowered by Your Holy Spirit today... Go before them now, Lord, so everyone around them may see the mighty things we can do when You are with us. Bless them, I pray in Jesus' name. Amen.

Day 5

Dear Heavenly Father, we come to You today, Lord, and we ask that You would renew and revive us, Father. We ask that You would fill us with Your living water so that You restore the dry places in our hearts and minds. Sometimes life just seems to drain us to the point that we have nothing left to give and we feel parched and dry inside. Lord, that is when we need to come to You and ask You to pour out Your Spirit. Fill us now, we pray, Lord.

Father, help us today to live for You... Help us to cast aside negative feelings and emotions. Help us to find relief from the stress of life. Life can seem like a winding path. We can't see around the bends and curves... We can't always see what's coming... We can't always know that relief is right around the corner... But You see all these things, Lord. We ask for You to lead us and guide us. We ask to know You better, so we can trust You more for the things we can't see and for the things that seem delayed. May our love for You deepen and may we be content to take small steps and wait patiently while You work in us.

Lord, we give You all we have, good and bad, and lay it on Your altar. Please, rain down Your grace and mercy this day, Lord. We praise You and lift Your name on high for You are our provider and strength. Amen.

Day 6

Dear Lord, we come and we ask for You to lead us to a place of stillness and calmness today. Please, lead us to that place that is a safe harbor from the loudness of the world. A quiet place from the demands that are on us. Take us to that place where we can hear Your voice above all others, as we seek Your guidance and direction for all that lies before us.

Lord, calm anxious minds. We ask for strength and to be steadfast so we can rebuke the enemy when he tries to discourage us and tell us that there is no hope... When he tries to tell us that things will never get better... When he tries to make us our own worst enemy with our thinking... Sometimes we don't need to be attacked from without, as our own minds attack us from within. Help us to hold every thought captive and to meditate on Your Word.

To think the enemy tried tempting Jesus... That he would lie to Your Son, is beyond comprehension, yet he did... So we know we will remain targets. But we also know how the story ends and we are victorious even if he is relentless in his pursuit of us. Help us to remember we are in a battle for our souls. All the things that happen to us... They are distractions that the enemy would seek to use to draw us away from You. Help us stand strong... Not by our strength, but with Yours. We are equipped with the truth of Your Word, proclaiming him a liar, a thief and defeated!!!

So many times we give up, Lord. We get tired. We get discouraged. We look at the doom and gloom in the world and we think "who am I that things should be different for me?" But we know Whose we are... We are Yours! No one can take that away from us, ever!! And when the bullies of life and those who seek to see us fail and fall come after us, help us to remember Who has our back and Who is standing beside us saying "you'll have to come through Me to get to My child." Lord, help us with visual pictures... Help us see these things in our mind to make the truth more real.

Lord, today as we go forth with all that is before us, help us to remember that You speak and waves and winds stop. Help us to remember that You set the captives free... Not only from sin and death, but You sent Your angels to free Your disciples in prison. You closed the mouth of lions. You caused the flames to not consume Your three children who would not bow down to the world. You parted the Red Sea when Your children needed to escape.

You made an endless supply of oil for a needy widow who gave generously even when she had little... That's who our Abba-Father is... That's Who stands behind us, that's Who goes before us... The Great I Am, Who has known us before we were born and Who calls us by name. We are important to You and we matter. Thank You, Lord.

For every discouraged heart that is praying; for every weary parent who has struggled to do everything right, yet everything is going wrong; for every anxious heart that awaits news of healings and help and provision; for everyone who wonders when the pain will stop and when they will feel whole again. Renew their hope, Father. Renew their strength. Renew and confirm in their hearts, which way to proceed on the path You have before them. Help them to remember that we are in this world, but not of it and that we are just passing through on our way to far better things.

Please, meet each heart where they are at, Lord, and help them to see signs of You in their busy days. Help them to see Your handiwork that declares Your glory and greatness. Help them to feel and sense, with full assurance, they are not alone, for You are with them and they are so loved by You. In Jesus' name we pray, Amen.

Day 7

Dear Lord, we come before You and we thank You for this day. Thank You, Lord, for Your love and compassion that sees past our weakness and our failures. Thank You, Lord, that You look on us, mindful that we are but dust, but You still call us Your children.

Lord, we ask that You would forgive us of our sins. Cleanse us this day, and make a right spirit within us. Help us to overcome those things that so easily stumble us and keep us from being all that You want us to be.

Lord, I ask for all those that are feeling broken, that You would reach down and pick up the pieces of their shattered hearts. For those whose hearts are aching and in pain, who feel like it's an effort to just get out of bed being so bogged down with worries and cares and grief... Lord, we call on Your Name and ask for physical strength... For physical healing... For emotional healing... Lord, lift the dark veil of sadness and grief and let the light of Your truth shine in the dark places... Let Your light shine on those places of darkness that they have been afraid to share with others... The dark places of shame and guilt... And whether it's caused by something they've done or something that's been done to them... Lord, we pray that they will find freedom... Freedom to know, believe and accept that You died to set them free. The enemy longs to see us rendered useless and he will feed us lies that deceive us... We ask that You break those chains today, Lord... Break the chains of thought that say they are not good enough... The lie that says they will never get better... The lies that say they are not lovable, or good looking enough. Break the chains of addictions, and poverty, and anger, and judgment. Lord, we pray for freedom... For the freedom that is our entitlement as Your children... not because of anything we have done but because of the saving, freeing power that You bought for us when You died for us and rose again... Lord, we pray for miracles in this place and in these hearts.

Lord, You want only the best for Your children. You have so much that awaits each one. Help them not to settle for anything less than Your best in their lives, in every area. Let each one rise up with the Power that lives within... The Power of Your Holy Spirit... and by that Power, let them feel and know that this is a new day... A new beginning... A day to begin living the changes that will lead to freedom and peace and joy... The joy that the enemy cannot steal or take away from them... Let this be the day that leads to victory in their lives... You are raising

Your children up, Lord... You are strengthening them and encouraging them, reminding them that there is healing, there is peace and there is revival coming and we pray that they will feel and know that they can do all things through Christ and that nothing is impossible through Him.

Lord, we ask You to come and fill each one now... Meet their needs and let them come and receive all that You have for them. We thank You and we praise You, Lord, for what You are going to do. In Jesus' name we pray, Amen.

Day 8

Dear Lord, we thank You for Your nearness. These are the times when we are better able to focus on You as we're free from distractions and we can feel Your presence. We thank You for that gift, Lord.

Father, I ask that You would be with each of my brothers and sisters. I ask that You would bless them and comfort them and assure them that they are not alone. I thank You for the works You are doing in each person. I know that You're just beginning Your work and You are faithful to complete it.

Lord, I know the enemy is not happy with those who are trying to do good and please You... For those who are making a stand and believing in Your Word. Father, I ask for Your hedge of protection about them. I ask, Lord, that You would stir up Your churches. Let them be the first, and the safest place we can go to when we are in need. Let our churches be emotionally healthy. Let them be filled with pastors that are filled with compassion and that teach their flocks to be the same way. I pray Your church... Your bride... would be a reflection of You. May there be people willing to stand in the gap and be in the trenches right alongside those who have problems that aren't cured with a quick fix. May all those who pray, believing, be healed and restored... Let them go forward as they are healed with a God-given desire to be an instrument of hope. May they comfort, with the comfort they've been given. Lord, if we all did that, what changes we would see around us!

Lord, for those praying, I ask that You would help them to be accepted and loved for who they are in You. I pray they would not be judged or condemned for their looks, for their income, for what they do or don't own, for any illnesses or injuries they have, or for anything that is buried in their past. Lord, for those single and lonely and longing for a mate, I ask that You would prepare them for each other and let them wait patiently until You bring them together. Help them not to give into loneliness... I pray they would not accept anything less than Your best for them. For those who are in bad relationships and bad marriages, I ask that You would do a mighty work. Please, bind the enemy and change hearts, so they will love You the most and then follow suit to love with Your love. Give them wisdom to know what Your will is and for those who are doing their part but their partner isn't, I ask for Your intervention, protection and peace to know Your will for them. Lord, I just ask for each person that has a hurting heart that they would be filled with hope and that You will heal their hurts and dry their tears.

For all the sick, for all the oppressed, for all the abused, neglected, disabled and financially strapped and weary, I ask for Your healing hand and Your hand of provision to be upon each one. We know nothing is too hard for You, Lord. Please, shower Your grace and mercy, filling each heart with peace and hope that You will restore all that they've lost. Please, give them a restful, peaceful weekend ahead, with moments in it that they can treasure. For all needs spoken and unspoken, we trust You, Lord, that You will meet them in Your time. Thank You, Lord, for hearing our prayers and we thank You for what You are about to do. In Jesus' name, Amen.

Day 9

Dear Lord, today, what keeps coming to my mind is the bride of Christ... You tell us in Your Word, that the Church is Your bride. And that may seem so strange to people... But it is actually a wonderful vision. When we think of what a bride represents in her dress, she represents purity. She is beautiful, lovely and adored. To be a bride is something that most women look forward to with excited anticipation. They dream about that day. It consumes their thoughts. The wedding day for a couple to be united in marriage is something that is looked forward to as one of the biggest events of their lives. Lord, I ask that You would give us a vision today of being united with You. May we have a sense of longing for the day in which we will be with You... Pure and white... Cleansed from sin and the scars of this world... Lovingly adorned and adored, with a love that is so utterly consuming there is nothing in our world that can begin to compare to it. May we look forward to it with anticipation like a bride waits for her groom!

Lord, sometimes life is such a struggle. People turn out to be different from the way we thought they would be. Life turns out differently than we thought it would be and we get discouraged. We get disappointed. We get stressed and wonder "when does it all end… When does the good stuff come?" Lord, help us to remember that the best is yet to come. Just like You turned the water to wine and You saved the best for the last, that is how it is going to be for us… The very best moments we have had in this life are nothing compared to that moment when we come before You and we feel Your embrace… When we look into the eyes that have loved us with an everlasting love that surpasses anything we have ever known.

Lord, help us to keep that vision in our mind when we are facing our struggles and hard times. May we be recharged and re-energized knowing that You are waiting for us with eager anticipation, like a bride groom waits for his bride. On that day, all the heartache and pain will fade in that instant as we lay eyes on You and when we feel You embrace us with Your nail-pierced hands. Oh, what joy will fill our hearts! Thank You, Lord… We are so unworthy, but You see us white and unblemished. You are so worthy of our praise. We give You today and all that's in it. May we find the moments of joy that come from You and help us to press on, looking forward to that great day that awaits us all. In Jesus' name we pray, Amen.

Day 10

Dear Lord, I lift up all those to You who are stuck in uncertainty. Please, bring comfort and acceptance to all those who are left trying to figure out why their spouses left; for those struggling to understand why people have turned their backs when they were needed most; for those watching as loved ones struggle with addictions and they can't understand why they can't just walk away from it. Please, speak to those who are struggling in their relationship with You because they don't understand why their prayers haven't been answered yet.

Please, bring peace and acceptance to those who are wondering why their loved ones are sick when they are good people; for those who are wondering why their adversity never seems to end. Lord, I know we will never have all of our "why" questions answered in this lifetime. Lord, please, help us to accept what we can't change. Lord, please, help each one to know that You do give us more of Yourself to fill those blank spaces where we want answers.

Lord, I ask for Your peace and Your comfort to rain down on us as we pray. I ask that You will help us find release and peace. May we feel Your presence and may we find that place where we can say "I don't understand, but I will trust You, Lord." We can't control the actions of others. We can't make people see the truth. We can't make people do the right thing or be the right thing... Only You can do that, Lord. The fact of the matter is, You are a gentleman and You never impose Your will on anyone. People have free will and free choice and sometimes they choose wrongly and we can only pray that they will see the light of truth someday. Please, help us to remember these truths when we are anxious for Your intervention.

Please, watch over us. Speak to our hearts. Move in our lives. Let us see, no matter what is in front of us, that You are with us and that You will go before us. May we know that You move mountains and smooth rough roads, and open doors and lead and guide us. May we get to that place of trust and acceptance that can only be found in You.

Lord, I ask that You would break the chains this day... Let them release the "why" to find THE WHO... You, Lord. You are the One who will help us feel whole and complete when nothing else will. You will help us trade our questions for hope and peace. Bless us all, I pray, Lord. Help us so we can move on beyond the questions to the place beyond grief to healing. In Jesus' name, Amen.

Day 11

Dear Heavenly Father, we gather together in prayer once again to feel Your presence and to bring our needs before You. Lord, we know that You know our needs, whether we pray them out loud or not. You want us to pray so we can experience You and Your power. You long to draw Your children into Your presence and to hold us close and to tell us "I'm here and I'm listening"... You are our Abba-Father... The one that loved us before we were formed in the womb... You know us by name and You have us engraved on the palm of Your hand. We never leave Your thoughts and what a comfort that is, Lord.

You never grow faint or weary and You never grow tired of us coming to You with petitions or questions or just to talk so we can feel You are near. Lord, I ask as we are praying now that we will feel the presence of Your Holy Spirit. I ask that You will fill us with Your peace that passes our human understanding. I ask that You would calm any anxious feelings and take away all fear and stress.

Father, please, hold those who are crying and grieving close to Your chest and let them feel a sweet release as their tears fall. I pray Father, in the quietness of their rooms that they would bring You their questions and their anger and all the things that they don't understand. Let them picture You sitting there beside them, listening patiently and attentively to their frustrations, worries and cares. I pray that they would not be afraid to let loose of the emotions that they've kept bottled inside. Let them come boldly to Your throne of grace, where You cast none aside.

Lord, You know the hard, painful stuff that they keep pent up. The stuff they are afraid to let go of, for fear that they will never stop crying once they start. Lord, I ask for healing... Release and healing from the grief and the sadness and the loneliness and the anguish that comes from the "whys" and the "if onlys." Help them to let go, Lord. For all those who are ill... For all those whose loved ones are ill. Lord, please, rain down Your grace and let them know You are there and with them in the dark hours of their souls.

Lord, there are many that are facing perilous futures because of lack of money... They don't know where they're going to live. They don't know how they're going to pay their bills. They need to go to the doctor and they don't have money to go. You see each one that is filled with worry and how they are feeling inadequate and the devil would like to tell them they are failures. They need to know from You, that is a lie from the pit. Lord, You allow all these things so we will learn to come to You... So we will come like a little child and say, "Daddy, I'm scared... Daddy, I don't understand... and Daddy, please, fix this because I can't."

Lord, we are asking for miracles in Jesus' name. By His stripes we are healed, and by Your Word, manna comes down from Heaven... By Your Word, the Red Sea parts and we are delivered from our enemies. Lord, I ask for You to do miracles so people can see that You are the One, true, living God and there is no one before You or like You. I ask for miracles, so we can gather together and say, "this is what my Heavenly Father did for me." I ask for miracles, so we can proclaim to the world, that You are alive and real... and You do hear our cries... and You do see our needs... and You are faithful and just, to fulfill them according to Your will and in Your time. Lord, You tell us that all we need is the faith of a mustard seed and I am asking that You help those who have unbelief. Help those who have given up... Those who think, "what's the point in praying?" Father, let them see You work like never before, so they will renew their faith. Lord, for every other need that exists right now, I ask that You would meet those as well. Thank You,

Lord. Thank You, for what You're going to do. Thank You, for this one You've gathered to read this and to join as one in prayer. We are one in You. When one part of the body hurts, we all hurt. So, Lord, we lift up all the hurting and pray for Your blessing on them and then we will rejoice with them, when they receive a touch from You. We thank You, Lord. We praise You. We trust and believe You, Lord. Go before us now we pray, in Jesus' name, Amen.

Day 12

Father, today we ask that You would help us to let go of our stress. There is just so much stress every day and sometimes we just feel like we will be crushed under the weight of it. We pray for Your help and we ask that You will hear as we lift up the many needs in our lives…

Lord, please, help those today with heavy work loads and long hours…

Lord, please, help those who are struggling with difficult relationships or are dealing with misunderstandings…

Lord, please, help those who have cars that need repair, but don't have the funds to fix them. They are in such a bind…

Lord, please, help those who are needing medical help and can't afford it…

Lord, please, help those who are battling depression and grief and so their stress threshold is diminished…

Lord, please, help those who are looking for work and can't find a job…

Lord, please, help all the single parents who just struggle through each day with too much to do and not enough help…

Lord, please, help the ones that are caregivers, spouses and parents of those with special needs…

Lord, please, help all those who are in financial straits and they've exhausted all their options and they are looking towards You as their only hope…

Lord, we ask for all those who struggle with addictions and we pray for the loved ones of those who struggle with addictions…

Lord, for all those who are battling health issues themselves or who have loved ones who are… Lord, I know there are so many who are dealing with multiple things at once… Please, Lord, refresh and carry them today when they are weary and overwhelmed. Carry them through the dark valley till they reach the other side!

Lord, I know the list is endless of the things that cause us stress. Our world is so much more complex and difficult to live in nowadays, but though the world crumble around us, You are our Rock. You are our Security. You are our Redeemer and You are the Constant in our lives that never changes. Lord, we trust You and we seek to obey You and Your commandments. Please, cleanse us, Lord, and if there be anything in our lives that is hindering our prayers, we ask that You would show it to us, Lord. We want to be in Your will, Father! We thank You for never growing tired or weary, and Lord, we thank You for hearing us and believing in us, Lord. In Jesus' name, Amen.

Day 13

Dear Lord, we have felt at times, like You haven't seen our plight.

We have felt at times, that You have turned Your back on us.

We have felt at times, that we have carried trouble with no aid.

We have felt at times, that the godless have thrived.

We have felt at times, that those same people have looked on us with contempt.

So, today we throw ourselves into Your care.

Even if we can't see how You care for us today, we trust that You do. When we think back, we can see the ways You have been good to us. So, we surrender our lives to You today, Lord. Keep our whole beings fixed on You. Let our minds recall Your Word and promises. Cleanse and purify our minds.

Lord, You tell us in Your Word that there is nowhere that we can go, that You are not there. You tell us that no good thing, will You withhold from those that love You... Increase our faith, Lord.

Please, heal our hurts and help us to move forward and get past all those things that keep us from being who You want us to be... that keep us from being where You want us to be.

Watch over those we love and meet their every need.

Thank You, Lord, that You do know what we need before we even ask. Be our strength when we are weak. Please, send Your comfort and ease our anxious thoughts. Please, go before us this day. In Jesus' name, Amen.

Day 14

Dear Lord, we come today and we ask, first of all, for everyone who is hurting in the world today because they have lost a loved one to senseless violence. We ask that You would comfort them, Lord, as they grieve and mourn. Father, we ask for Your hedge of protection about Your children. We ask for Your hedge of protection about our children, Lord.

So many things are being overtaken in the world by evil. We see so many changes in our lives in just the last twenty years... Children can't feel safe at school because of shootings, we are searched and go through so much at airports... And now innocent people go to a movie and don't come home... And there is so much more. Every day it seems we lose something else that we took for granted for so long. I know there are many parts of the world that live with much uncertainty in life, whether they are sitting in their home or a corner cafe... We are losing our sense of safety, Lord, and we need Your reassurance and peace.

I pray for all those who are fearful and anxious. Lord, every day we turn on the news or look at the paper, we see this world in a state of turmoil and anarchy. Lord, we pray now that we would not succumb to fear. We ask that You would help us to keep our eyes focused intently on You and not what is going on around us, Lord. You tell us, we will see wars and hear rumors of wars. We will see family members turning against family members. You tell us, there will be famines and natural disasters and we are seeing it all unfold right before our eyes.

Lord, these times are not for the weak of heart and as our hearts break for those who suffer, we can only imagine how Your heart grieves. Lord, give us strength and courage to keep pressing on. Help us to lean into You and to turn to each other so we can pray for each other and lift each other up. May we be able to encourage everyone we come in contact with and may we in turn be encouraged. Help us to keep our hearts and minds steadfast in You... For every day that is filled with heartache, we must remember it is also bringing us one day closer to being with You.

Lord, please, be with my friends and meet their every need. Watch over them and keep them safe from harm. Heal their bodies and provide for their needs, Lord. But most importantly, give them grace to endure and help them not to grow weary in well-doing. Help them grow in knowledge of Your Word and engrave Your promises on their hearts. Help them to keep their eyes on the prize and remember all the heartache and heartbreak in this world is temporary and we are only passing through. Give each of them a great weekend with peaceful, relaxing moments so they can re-charge. We love You, Father. We thank You for hearing our prayers. In Jesus' name, Amen.

Day 15

Dear Lord, I lift my friends to You today and I ask that You would strengthen their faith today, Lord. I ask that You would encourage them and infuse them with hope today. Help them to hold on, Lord. I think of the words in "Before the Morning" and there is so much truth in that song, Lord. Everything we are feeling and dealing with here, is just the dark before the morning. The light is coming and the victory is won. We know how the story ends and someday, we will see the bigger picture of our lives. None of this drama and tragedy is for nothing. Help them to believe that there is a purpose to their pain.

Lord, You tell us when we get to Heaven, You will dry our tears... That means we must go through pain, loss and difficulties here or why else would You be drying our tears? Help my friends to get a mental picture in their minds of their Savior tenderly wiping away the tears from their eyes. What an intimate moment that will be, where You show Your care and affection for us. Oh, Lord, help us to press in and to cling to You so that we can hear You say to us one day, "Well done, good and faithful servant... You fought the good fight and I am so proud of You!"

Lord, I pray for those who are struggling to let go of hurts. I pray for those who do not want to accept the things that have happened and because of that refusal, they stay trapped in their pain. Oh, Lord, I pray they will find the strength to allow You to let their pain be useful to them. Help them to dare to trust You and believe that a better day awaits them. Father, I have seen countless times how You have turned tragedy to triumph and I know You intend that for each of my friends. Build their faith, Lord. Encourage them. Grow them. Nurture them. Bless them with glimpses of things to come. May they sense Your presence this day and may they feel Your hope and peace. Things may not get better today or tomorrow, but the dawn is coming after their dark days and we praise You and we thank You in advance, Lord, for the fulfillment of that promise. In Jesus' name we pray, Amen.

Day 16

Dear Lord, I think of how often, in the midst of our dark days, we can find incredible beauty... Yet we don't focus our attention on that... Our attention is usually focused on the darkness that surrounds us. Lord, help us to retrain our thinking so we will see all the things we can be thankful for in the midst of our trials... Help us to find the blessings that are hidden in disguise.

Help us to be excited that even through our trials, we will get to know You in ways we could not know You in the good times...

Help us to recognize that the pressure from our trials is changing us from a diamond in the rough, to a beautiful gem in Your masterful hand...

Help us to realize that with the changes that take place in our lives, it means You are putting us on a new path that will lead to something good that we can't yet imagine...

Help us to see that in the midst of adversity, we learn our true strength... It's not by our might or our power, but by Yours...

Help us to be watchful and mindful, so we look beyond ourselves and our pain and worry, to see You answer prayers and do miracles in our midst....

Lord, please, give us "night vision" to help us see as You do in the darkness. Help us not to have tunnel vision that only sees what is right in front of us, but instead, help us to see the "bigger picture." Help us to not grow complacent or to stay stagnant in our place of pain. Help us to make the most of our days, so we can experience all we can of You while we are here, Lord.

Help our lives to count... Help our lives to matter... Help us to experience the fullness of joy that comes from You and to taste and see that You are good, even in the midst of our darkest days. Thank You, Lord, that all things are possible through You and that nothing is impossible for You! Worthy are You to be praised, our Lord and King. Amen.

Day 17

Dear Lord, today we focus on You and Who You are. I think of that saying, "don't tell God how big your problems are, tell your problems about how big your God is." So, Lord, today we thank You that You are bigger than anything we will ever face. Help us to remember that You are...

The Alpha and Omega, the beginning and end. Through You and by You, everything came into being. There is no one greater than You, Lord.

You are the Bread of Life... You came down from Heaven to be our sustenance, so we should never hunger or thirst.

You are the Light of the World... With You we need never lose our way. You are the light in the darkness, always leading, guiding us.

You are The Lamb that was slain... The Holy One, Who died to save us from a debt we could never pay. You are The One that conquered sin and death... There is no one mightier than You, our Lord and Savior.

You are The Great Physician, and You alone can heal our broken hearts, and bind our wounds, and heal our infirmities and heal us from the inside out.

You are our Strength, our Shield, our Fortress, our Deliverer, our very present Help in times of trouble... What can man do to us, Lord? For surely we are safe and secure and protected in Your care....

Oh, Lord, there is so much more that You are... We could be here all day, just praising You as we think of all of Your names... But as we meditate on all that You are, we truly realize You are the Prince of Peace... Our peace of mind comes from You. Our sense of peace in the storms comes from You... The peace that You give is not as this world gives, it passes all understanding.

May we carry all that You are in our hearts today, Lord. May every trial, every pain, every need pale in comparison and shrink in size, when we think on You today, Lord. We know we are loved, safe, provided for and empowered by You. We thank You, Lord, for all these things and for all You are. Amen.

Day 18

Dear Lord,

We want to just stop and thank You for waking us up today. Thank You, for all that You do for us. Thank You, for all the subtle little things You do in our day to make us aware that You are with us and thinking of us. You are always aware of what's going on with us and mindful of our needs.

Our Precious Savior, we can never repay You. We could never be worthy enough, but You don't ask these things of us. You, in Your gracious love, just ask us to receive You and believe You…This is truly the most gracious gift we could ever receive… To believe and spend all eternity with You.

Thank You, Lord, that our lives and eternity are not about our worthiness, or our strength or our love… It's all about Yours. Thank You, Lord, for the many prophecies Your birth and death fulfilled. Thank You, that Your Word and promises are true. Thank You, that You made a way where there was no way! You, our Lord, are so worthy to be praised.

Lord, for all those who are in need of hope, today may they be reminded that if You were able to conquer sin and death, You surely can help them overcome their difficulties. There was darkness the day You died... And just as surely as You turned that around and shined the light of truth into this dark, dreary world... You are waiting to shine Your light of truth and love in each believer's life. We have hope, and we have a future, and we have a Savior and we are more than conquerors through You. By Your stripes we are healed. And at the mention of Your name, evil must flee. You promise to provide and deliver and redeem and restore. You, our Lord, are our everlasting hope and the answer to our every hurt and need.

We praise You, Lord, for Who You are and for all that You do in our lives. No matter how bleak things look for us from a worldly perspective, we know that it's the eternal perspective that matters. You see things so differently than we do... We lose sight of just how short our time here is and what things in our lives really have eternal value. May we learn to count it all joy and to treasure our days. May we not let people, things or circumstances get us down or keep us from focusing on the journey before us.

Every day we seek and ask, Lord. Today we just want to thank You, and praise You and rest in You. You know our needs and that is enough. We come before You to take in Your presence and to be filled with Your joy. We love You, Lord, and we are so grateful for everything You do for us. In Jesus' name we pray, Amen.

Day 19

Dear Father God, we come to You and we thank You, Lord, that You never grow tired or weary. We thank You, Lord, that You are never late or early. You never forget. You never miss one thing that is going on in our lives. Lord, I know there are many praying right now who are discouraged and losing hope...

For all the ones who are weary with physical pain...

For all the ones who are down to their last dollar and they don't know where the next meal is coming from...

For all the ones who are trapped in a cycle of financial difficulty they can't escape from...

For all the ones who have done everything they can and they are still estranged from loved ones...

For all those who have lost their loved ones and they just don't know how to function with the all-consuming grief and loss...

For all those who have had just one bad thing piled on top of another and they feel that life is just too hard... That they don't have any more strength and they are just too weary to keep trying...

For all those who prayed and believed and still their prayers were unanswered and they are riddled with doubt and confusion...

Lord, right now, for all of these, we pray for miracles, Father God. We ask, first of all, for Your peace that passes all understanding... We ask that for where they are right now. May they feel the warmth of Your Spirit descend upon them. We ask for the stress to leave their bodies. We ask that they will feel, with each exhaled breath, a calmness that overtakes them that can only be attributed to You. Lord, it may not be time for their circumstances to change yet, but we know You can change each person so they can find the strength and ability to hold on until You move mountains for them. We know, sometimes, You want them to come to the end of their strength, so they will find You with open arms... Oh, Abba-Father, hold them close to You right now, please.

Lord, each one praying is earnestly seeking You. They are seeking Your will and Your strength and Your courage. Lord, we ask that Your heart would be moved with compassion, as a father's is, when his child is in pain. Lord, We are asking for miracle provisions for those in need. We believe with all our hearts, that You are the God, who with one word, can speak the world into existence. We know that with one word or thought, every need can be met here. We ask for Your will to be done. We will praise You and glorify Your name, for all that is done here, in the name of Jesus.

Lord, we ask that You embrace us... Encourage us... Empower us... Deliver us. Make our hearts Your home. Dwell within us and fill us, with Your sustaining grace. Lord, please, give each one here the strength and power to hold on for one more day. That's all we need... Just one day at a time. Your grace is sufficient for this day. May they feel it, may they know it, may they sense it... That You are with them this day and they are not alone. They are not weak. They are strong in You and this day, You have equipped them for all they will face today. Thank You, Lord. In Jesus' name we ask and receive, Amen.

Day 20

Dear Lord, we come to You and we pray for all those who are struggling today. We ask, in Jesus' name, that You will be with each person who is struggling with addiction... Whether it be alcohol, drugs, sex, gambling, pornography, food or even the need to be needed. Some are dealing with more than one addiction at a time. Lord, You are our Deliverer. We can do anything through Christ who strengthens us... But we must take the first step. We must realize we have a problem and a need and we must ask for help. I ask, Lord, that You will give each one the courage to face up to their problems and to have a strong desire to change.

We ask that You will remove all outside influences that hinder them from coming clean, who perpetuate their addictions. We ask, in Jesus' name, that You will bind the enemy and that You will put Your angels about each person to protect them from themselves and from the things that keep dragging them down. Lord, we know many self-medicate so they won't have to deal with pain or memories that overshadow their lives. We pray that You will give them the courage and the strength to face down their demons and hurts and to clean out the wounds once and for all, so they can be free to be the person that You've called them to be... To be free from the sickness and pain that keeps them in bondage.

Lord, we ask for deliverance... for that life changing freedom they can find in You, Lord. We ask for healing, in families torn apart by addiction. We ask for protection, for those family members that are in harm's way, because of their loved one's destructive ways. Lord, everyone suffers in a family where there is addiction. Please, pour out Your grace and healing power on each person who is, or who has been, affected by someone in their life that has an addiction.

May the chains be broken right now, Lord. Set the captives free and please, begin that healing that only You can bring. Please, bring hope. Give a vision of what life can be, as a person freed from the pain and addiction. Lord, for every need spoken or hidden, You know them all and we ask for Your provision.

Please, bring helpful people into their lives that will stand beside them and help them to be accountable to stay clean and free. May You restore their sense of self-worth. May they find redemption and restoration in You, Lord. We praise You and we thank You, Lord, for the work You are going to do. In Jesus' name we pray, Amen.

Day 21

Dear Lord, we come to You and we lift up those who are broken-hearted because of infidelity and betrayal. There are so many that are struggling, searching for reasons why things went wrong in their relationships. Lord, for those who are wondering what happened to the person they knew, please, replace the questions with peace. For those who are wondering how a person could change so much, help them to realize and accept, there are just some things we will never know or understand in this life.

For those who have been crushed by lies and deceit and hurtful words, we ask that You would heal the wounds and help them to find their worth in You. For those who are forced to see their loved ones move on with someone else, please, comfort them, Lord, as only You can. Please, Lord, replace the longing that they have for things to be the way they used to be. May they find the courage to accept what they can't change. You are with them, walking this hard road. For the times when they just hurt and they long to return to the life and love they knew, give them strength to look forward without looking back. Help them to be free. Help them to see themselves as over-comers and not just victims to this person's sin.

Lord, we know they long for answers and they want to know why they "weren't enough" for the person they loved... Help them to see this wasn't about them or their inadequacies, it was about their mate and their problems. Sometimes, there are things we could change that would have helped, but with some people, it wouldn't matter if we did absolutely everything right, it would still have ended up with the same result. Lord, please, take away the feelings of failure and inadequacy.

Lord, for all those who now find themselves starting over and in financial difficulties, we ask that You would provide for them. May they find a new trust in You to know that You will look after them. For those who are forced to see their children split up in visitation and custody issues... We pray for the children and we ask for Your protection over them and healing for them. Please, comfort the parents who must now split their time. Please, comfort them when their children are forced to go, when they would rather stay with them. Lord, there are so many issues that come up... So many losses at once, when a family is torn apart. This is never how You intended things to be, Lord, but we live in a fallen world. Please, comfort and protect those You love, Father... Oh, Lord, please, comfort them all.

Lord, divorce was never part of Your plan... It's not something You want, but there is sin in the world and free will and Satan lurks around trying to wreak havoc and destruction. For any marriages that are able to be restored, we ask for that restoration miracle and for You to move mountains and change hearts and bring forgiveness. Please, heal memories and please, restore all that the enemy has tried to destroy and take away. But for those who are dealing with their spouse whose heart is hardened towards You and towards them, we ask for deliverance. Please, release them from their feelings, so they can move forward with their eyes focused on You... and not what was in the past, but the new road that You have before them. Lord, for those who have lost loved ones and friends in the wake of divorce, we ask that You will bring others to stand beside them... to love and encourage them. For the lonely nights, we pray that You will be so real and so present. Lord, when two are joined together, You meant for them to be one and it hurts when that unit is torn apart, but You are our Healer, Lord. You are near to the broken-hearted and You bind their wounds. You see each tear, You hear each cry, and You are able to do everything we can't, Lord. Give them courage. Give them strength. Fill them with love from You, which is more fulfilling than any human's love. Help them to heal after grieving and help them to find restoration in Your loving arms. Go before them and protect them in every way and may they feel in their hearts and minds that there is hope because of You. Bless each one, Lord, we pray, in Jesus' name, Amen.

Day 22

Dear Lord, we ask that You would help make us people after Your own heart. We thank You, Lord, for the work You are doing in each of us. We thank You, for forgiving us of our sins and that You remember them no more. We thank You, that You are healing our hurts and binding our wounds... That You are making a way in the wilderness for us.

We ask, Lord, that You would help us not to judge others. We are reminded that You said, "He who is without sin, cast the first stone." Some of us have many secrets and hurts tucked away deep inside our hearts... Others, live in metaphorical glass houses where everything is on display for the world to see and it's not always pretty. We thank You, Lord, that You see past all of that to how we're going to be... Shaped into the likeness of The One, Who loves us so.

Help us all, Lord, to lay all the things down that hold us back and keep us from fulfilling the plan that You have for us. Set us free to hear the song that You placed inside each of us, and may our lives be as a symphony of praise to You.

We pray that You would kindle a fire in each of us so that we will want more of You... and deeper fellowship with You. Help us not to waste another day, longing for what once was, or what could have been. Help us not to compare ourselves with others, or to put ourselves down, thinking that we are not worthy or good enough. Help us to remember our divine inheritance and may Your light shine brightly in us and through us.

We trust that You will heal those who are hurting and that You will provide for those in need. We know You promise to turn our mourning to joy, Lord. We long to dance before You as David did. Our hope is in You, Lord, and we sing Your praises this day, as we wait on You to fulfill Your promises to us. With love and gratitude, we pray in Jesus' name, Amen!

Day 23

Dear Lord, as we come together, Father, I pray for encouragement. Father, for everyone who is discouraged and feeling weary, I pray that You would be the lifter of their heads. I pray that You would let Your joy and Your grace rain down on them and refresh them, Lord. I pray for those who feel shame. I ask that You would release them and help them to not be held captive by their past or by abusive, hurtful words that robbed them of their sense of self-worth.

Lord, for every one that has been told they should just "get over" their grief... For everyone who has been made to feel that the bad things that have happened to them are their own fault, I pray that You would take away the sting of clueless words and actions. For everyone who has been told to "just suck it up" and "quit crying..." speak healing to them and let them know that grief, and crying, are a normal and natural response to loss.

Oh, Lord, bring Your healing balm to these wounded hearts and minds. Break the tape that repetitively plays these destructive things in their brains. Replace those images and words with truth that comes from You, Lord.

I pray for those who have bought into the lies of society, that make them feel like they are failures, because they do not lead the life that others consider successful. I pray for those who think because they are single or divorced, that there must be something wrong with them. I pray for each person, who has suffered at the hands of verbal bullies taunting them with distorted and misplaced truth. Oh, Lord, set each one free from the pain and the chains that have been placed on them. For those who have felt that they don't live up to what they should look like by the media's standards... And for those who had that reinforced by rejection, please, help their self-esteem, Lord. Help them to realize You make everyone in Your own likeness and You do not make mistakes.

Lord, I pray for every person that is verbally, mentally, or emotionally abusive. May they find their way to You and see a need for You, so that their ways will change. I pray for all the loved ones who whose painful ways are fueled by addictions. Please, set them free, Lord, and deliver them so there can be healing for all.

Lord, part of Your restoration and healing process is to heal damaged emotions and hurt feelings. We know we are all works in progress and we can only work on one thing at a time, but I pray You would bring healing in this area now, Lord. Restore all those who are emotionally damaged and walking around with a wounded sense of self-worth. May we see the love of Jesus shining forth in each other and recognize that beauty when we meet. May our words bring healing and encouragement to others. In Jesus' name we pray, Amen.

Day 24

Dear Lord, thank You, for this day! We give You our fears, our worries and our concerns. Father, please, grant us Your wisdom, knowledge and discernment about what we're facing. Please, give us insight from Your Word about what we're facing. God, may we sense Your presence today, and every day and in everything.

All that we are, Lord, we place into Your hands.

All that we do, Lord, we place into Your hands.

Everything we work for, we place into Your hands.

Everything we hope for, we place into Your hands.

The troubles that weary us, we place into Your hands.

The thoughts that disturb us, we place into Your hands.

The financial burdens we face, we place into Your hands.

Our loved ones who are in need, we place into Your hands.

The troubled relationships we have, we place into Your hands.

Our grief, our longings, our need for physical and mental restoration, we place into Your hands.

We place into Your hands, Lord, the choices that we face. Guard us from choosing the wrong things which will take us far from where You want us to be. Show us the way to the clear-cut path, that is safe and straight and that leads to You. Help us to find our happiness, in our acceptance of Your purposes for us. Lord, we give You this day and all that is within it, and place it into Your hands. In Jesus' name we pray, Amen.

Day 25

Dear Lord, we come together once again and we thank You, Lord, for being here for us. Lord, there is so much uncertainty in the world... Wars, economic downturn, trials... It can all be so overwhelming and it's so easy for all the cares and worries to overtake us so we are filled with anxiety and fear. Lord, I pray for all those that are feeling anxious or fearful. You tell us over and over again in Your Word, "fear not" and "be anxious for nothing." Lord, I know it's human to feel these things, and You know those feelings as well. You sweated drops of blood in Gethsemane; You know what it's like to be anxious for what lies ahead.

For those who have anxiety/panic disorders, their fear and anxiety rarely leaves. No matter how much they pray, it is always with them. So, Lord, I want to lift first the people with disorders that cause them to have anxiety, fear and stress... no matter how much faith they have. I pray for their healing, Lord. I ask that You would put Your healing hand upon them and touch them so their brain chemistry becomes balanced. I pray that their brains would be healed, so they might find relief. I pray the prayer of faith and ask believing, in the name of Jesus, for miracles for them, Lord.

Father, for those whose fear and anxiety is situational, I ask that You would eliminate their fear. Help them to cling to Your Word. Put that peace that passes all understanding in their hearts. I ask, Lord, that You would bind the enemy so that he can have no control in any areas of their lives, and especially in this one. Lord, as the days get worse and Your return draws near, help us to keep our eyes fixed on You and not the crumbling world around us. Let us cling to the hope that is ours as believers in Christ. Lord, give us renewed vision and strength. We believe that You give us blessings to strengthen us. You bring us all together as a community of believers, so we know we are not alone... So, we know that there is strength in numbers... So, we would know that You are still doing miracles, and that nothing is too hard for You.

We are encouraged, knowing that You are indeed in our midst and even though the enemy is roaming this earth seeking whom he may devour, You have not left us defenseless against his schemes. We declare he may not have access to any part of us.

You have given us Your Holy Spirit. You have given us an army of heavenly hosts who are fighting and protecting us. You have given us the body of Christ to intercede for one another. Lord, for the situations people are facing, such as death and illness, financial struggles, crumbling relationships, watching loved ones in painful situations... Lord, the fear is not some general feeling, but it's for something specific that is unfolding before eyes and in lives. I ask for Your divine intervention, Lord. Intercede on their behalf. Please, work as only You can.

Lord, I know You are working miracles... moving and orchestrating things unseen now, because they are behind the scenes. You are working things for our good and Your glory, Father. You tell us all we need is the faith of a mustard seed to move mountains and I am praying, and asking that You renew our strength. Strengthen our faith and give us hope to believe that You are there in the darkness and You will see us through to the light. Lord, let us see victory and wholeness, relief from burdens and cares. Go before us this day, Lord, and increase our confidence, that even though we may not see answers on the horizon, revelation is on the way... because You are working for our good. You promised and You are faithful. You are the same yesterday, today and forever. Your Word never fails and You will never let one of Your children stumble, if we are holding Your hand. I ask for Your peace to rain down on us right now, Lord, and please, remove all fear. In Jesus' name, the name above all names, we pray, Amen.

Day 26

Dear Lord, we come, today, asking for Your wisdom and discernment. We pray that You will help those who are filled with questions and doubts. We ask for guidance for those who just don't know which direction to go. We ask for those who have decisions to make and who are confused about what Your will is. Lord, I ask that You would speak to their hearts and minds. May they hear Your voice clearly above all others. I pray that You would make the rough roads smooth before them and close the doors You don't want them to go through. Please, open the one that is Your best choice for them and give them peace in their heart to confirm Your will.

Lord, for those who are praying, asking and seeking, yet they don't feel Your presence… I ask that they would find reassurance all around them, that You have not left them or abandoned them. Many times, our emotions hinder us from hearing Your voice and feeling Your presence. We contend with grief and numbness and things like shock after unexpected losses. It is normal for almost everyone to not feel much of anything during these times. I pray that You would give them glimmers of hope. I pray that You would light their way as they walk the dark path before them.

You never send us into the wilderness, Lord, without provision. You are faithful and true and if Your eye is on the sparrow, it is surely on us. Strengthen Your children, Father. May they find comfort by remembering the times You have delivered them in the past. May they find courage in Your promises for the future.

The enemy is constantly on the move trying to discourage and sidetrack us, Lord. We pray for each one... each household and each family and ask for Your hedge of protection about them. Bind the enemy so he has no room to work in our lives. We pray for Your blessing and for Your guardian angels to be about their homes and their loved ones. May they see with Your eyes of clarity and certainty, so they will not be deceived by the enemy's lies or schemes. We thank You, that we have a Savior that we can come to with all of our needs... In Jesus' name we pray, Amen.

Day 27

Dear Lord, what is on my heart as we pray is "courage." I pray Lord, that You will help each of us to be courageous in every area of our lives. I think of the men and women who founded the U.S.A. and how they were people of such amazing courage, faith and strength. They were willing to sacrifice everything they had, including their lives, for the pursuit of religious freedom and to live free from tyranny. Thank You, Lord, that there are still such people in this world today, who are willing to lay down their lives for their friends, family and country. May we never forget or take these sacrifices for granted.

Lord, there is so much in life that happens and we cannot face it without the courage which comes from You… Things like chronic illness, divorce, death, physical injury. Life can be so challenging at times and so hard to deal with. But we know with Your help and strength, there is no challenge that we cannot overcome. The enemy would so love to render us ineffective and useless. He would love to have us walk away defeated and discouraged. He would love for us to say there is no hope and to believe there is no use in trying. There is strength in numbers, Lord, and You are in the midst of us where two or more gather... So, Lord, we are looking for Your courage and strength today... Please, help us, Lord, in this quest for courage.

For the marriages that are on the verge of collapse and the spouses who know it would be easier to run than stand... Give them courage to cling to You and to commit their marriage to Your hands.

For the ones who are divorced and have to face life alone... For those who are having to start over and face the scary and overwhelming reality of this new life they didn't ask for... Give them courage, Lord. Let them see and feel that there is more to them and more for them in this life beyond their marriage. Let them find the courage to trust You and to take You at Your Word that You can heal and restore all that has been taken from them.

For the ones who are facing injury and illness... Give them the courage to not give up and not give in... We have to accept what we have, so we can deal with it... but we do not have to give in to it. We do not have to let those things define us. You can use us right where we are. You can use people like Joni Eareckson Tada, who is a quadriplegic, or Nick Vujicic, who has no limbs or a child with cancer or a mom with Fibromyalgia... Help each one to find the joy in the day and to fight courageously against hopelessness and despair. May they find the courage to face these things, knowing You have not abandoned them and You have a plan and a purpose in all things.

Lord, we ask for courage to face the uncertainty of our world. Help us to be fearless in the face of troubling economic times and collapse. Help us to go forward daily with the conviction and belief, that You are with us and that You see our needs and You are faithful to meet them. Help us to stand fast when we hear of wars and rumors of wars and every manner of natural disaster. May we stand, knowing that You are with us and You are ruler over all.

Lord, we ask for courage to face life without those we love. We are human and we can be weak and overwhelmed when we think of life without our loved ones. We know they would want us to soldier on without them. They would want us to rejoice that they are happy in Your presence and to carry on with our lives, treasuring the moments, as they pass all too quickly. Help each one praying to have the courage to press on and look up. Be their strength, Lord.

And finally, Lord, we ask for the courage to stand for You. Fill us with Your Holy Spirit and may we have Holy boldness to be witnesses for You. We know many are being persecuted around the world for their belief in You. We pray for them, Lord, and we ask that You would help us all to be unafraid, knowing that this life is temporary and not our home. Give us courage to speak Your truth in love and to point the way to You in all that we say and do.

Thank You, Lord, for always giving us what we need. Thank You, for all the brave people who have gone before us and been our role models of courage. We love You, Lord. We thank You and we praise You. In Jesus' name we pray, Amen.

Day 28

Dear Heavenly Father, we come to You today, thankful that You are the One that sustains us. Lord, sometimes our hearts are so heavy. We become so sad and barely able to function. Lord, for all those who find it difficult to rise out of bed because of the weight of their heavy hearts, I ask for the infusion of Your strength and energy. I ask that You would take their load from them and put Your healing balm upon their hearts.

Lord, for all those who are in the healing and helping professions... For those who, on a daily basis, deal with other people's pain, hurts, trauma and grief... For all the doctors, therapists, nurses, counselors, 911 operators, people who sit at suicide hotlines and 24-hour prayer numbers, the EMTs and paramedics, social workers, CPS workers, firefighters, safety, police and all who are in similar professions... Lord, we thank You for them. We thank You for the call that You have placed on these people's lives. Thank You, that they are able, day after day, to take on the problems of others - to offer help, healing and hope. We thank You for them, Lord, and ask that Your blessing be upon them. These are the people who keep our society running... The unsung heroes who deal with pain on a regular basis, in an effort to make a difference and bring help and hope. Renew their stores of strength, energy and compassion that they might carry on their necessary work.

Lord, I ask for Your sustaining power to fall on those who feel like they are merely surviving. I ask for those who have lost their joy... For those who are battle weary from dealing with one loss and one problem after another. I ask for refreshment for their souls, Lord. I ask for renewed hope and strength for the day. I ask for energy and friends to stand beside them to help carry their loads. Please, intercede on their behalf, Lord, and be everything they need today.

Lord, You know every heartbreaking story of every person praying. You know each one by name. You have a heart of compassion far greater than anything we can imagine. Lord, please, intervene... Please, heal and provide as only You can. Please, help those who have lost faith or never had any to begin with... Oh, Lord, I can only imagine the despair they feel trying to carry these things alone. I thank You that they have come here and I ask for miracles for them right now, Lord, and may they find the rest that comes from being Your child.

Lord, we come with open arms and say, "fill us, Lord. Fill us with Your Holy Spirit... Come, Lord... Take our burdens and cares... Come, Lord. We are ready for a movement by You in our lives... We are ready for You to break the chains that bind us physically, emotionally, financially, spiritually, mentally... Come, Lord. Show us the way in which we should go... Come, Lord. Fill us with Your peace that passes all understanding... Come, Lord. Kill off the old sinful nature in us that we might be conformed to Your image... Lord, we need You..." Without You we are lost and lonely children floundering in a troubled world with no sense of direction or purpose... With You, Lord, we have the key to every door and a path of purpose. Please, go before us. Please, move inside our hearts and minds and guard our hearts and minds in You, Lord, we pray. We give You ourselves and say "here I am Lord, not my will but thine. May we find rest and peace in You this day." Thank You, Lord, in advance, for what You are going to do. In Jesus' name, Amen.

Day 29

Our Dear Heavenly Father, we pray today for those who are struggling with their faith... For those who question how a loving God can allow pain and suffering. We lift up those who are angry, because they haven't seen You work the way they thought You should or would. We pray for all those who try to be faithful, but who stumble over the obstacles of adversity... For all those who are filled with doubts and questions... Lord, You know all and You see all, and You understand our humanness. You understand us, Lord, and You are filled with compassion. I ask that You would find a way to break through the blinders that keep these dear ones from knowing You and trusting You, with their whole hearts. I ask that You would speak to their hearts and let Your hope break through their pain, so they can see the truth and understand what is going on in their lives. We ask that You'd bind the enemy so he can't cause confusion. We ask that You speak truth and show mercy, so these will be drawn to You and Your unrelenting, compassionate love for them. We pray that each person will come to know You as their Lord and Savior and find the comfort that comes from being Your child.

Lord, I ask that You would help those praying to find freedom today. Help people to let go of grudges, hurts, bitterness and anger. I pray for those who are filled with sadness, depression, anxiety and fear and ask that You would help them to find relief and peace. Please, set people free from addictions and pain and illness and grief. May this be the day that a new dawn begins, Father. We trust You and believe in You and know that You are the God of miracles and nothing is too great or difficult for You.

Lord, for those who are feeling overwhelmed and defeated because they wait and pray and yet they are losing their houses, they have no money for food, they are without transportation and they feel like they are in an endless spiral that is going nowhere but down... Lord, we pray for miracles. We ask that You would honor their faith. We ask that You would intervene and provide in ways that no human could possibly do. We know Your promises are true and that Your children are taken care of by You, Father. Lord, please, don't let any of Your followers wonder how they are to feed, clothe or provide for their children or themselves. Please, help those parents who are struggling to provide... Help the ones that are dealing with health issues as well and all that are weary and see no relief on the horizon. Lord, God, please, intervene. I know You allow these trials for our good and so we can trust You... So, Lord, I pray each one will see You for who You are and will let go of fear and doubt, and trust You, knowing they will see Your goodness. Lord, please, meet every need, spoken or unspoken, and touch hearts and change minds and please, renew and restore what the enemy has stolen and destroyed. We lift these things in spirit, together, and thank You for hearing our pleas. In Jesus' name we ask these things. Amen.

Day 30

Father, we come to You and ask for Your help. We know that we are to forgive others as You have forgiven us, but we find it so hard to do, Lord. Our minds and hearts are full of anger for the things that have been said and done. At times it seems as though the ones that inflict pain and wounds are unrepentant... That they escape judgement. We are angry for what they have taken from us and for the pain they have caused us.

Lord, please, help us to see with Your eyes. Help us to remember that forgiveness is for us and not for them. Help us to remember that our forgiveness does not depend on them apologizing or repenting. Help us to remember that forgiveness is between us and You. Lord, we are releasing our pain and our hurt and our anger to You and we are asking for Your help in forgiving them, so we can be set free.

We want to forgive and leave this heavy weight at Your feet, so we can be set free. Lord, their sin and their wrong doing, we leave in Your hands for You to deal with. We no longer want to be held hostage in a prison of anger and bitterness and sadness, for what has been done by someone else. We no longer want to serve the sentence for what someone else has done wrong.

Lord, release us from this bondage and free our hearts. We forgive, Lord, as You have forgiven us. You died not only to set us free from our sins, but to set us free from all the things that hold us hostage and keep us from being who You want us to be... The things of this world that keep us from living in the peace and freedom that we can have in You.

Lord, from this day forward, we want to be healed from all these negative feelings. Thank You Lord, for helping us... What we can't do... What we don't have the strength to do on our own power, we know we are able to do through Jesus. We know that forgiving doesn't mean we have to trust or put ourselves in harmful, destructive relationships. Trust is earned and some people are not trustworthy. Forgiving just sets us free.

Thank You, Lord, for helping us to move forward today. Help our minds turn to You when the old feelings and thoughts start to enter our minds. Bind the enemy so he can't bring up the past. Clean the wounds out of our hearts, Lord, so they can finally heal and so we can be at peace. Thank You, Lord. In Jesus' name we ask all these things. Amen.

Day 31

Dear Lord God, we come together and we ask that You be in our midst. Lord, we are joining together in prayer, believing that Your Holy Spirit is with each one of us, Lord, and we are asking for You to speak to our hearts today.

Help us clear our minds of the hurts and pain we feel. Lord, help us to focus on You. Sometimes it's so hard because we do our best and it doesn't seem good enough. We do all we can to provide and we still fall short on finances as new things keep cropping up that are beyond our control. Help us to let go of the feelings that we are in control, because clearly we are not, Lord. You are! All You ask is we seek You and to do our best and leave the rest in Your hands. Help us, Father, to let go of our expectations and the expectations that others put on us. Help us to let go of the condemnation that we allow the enemy to pile on us. We ask You to help us overcome in this area, Lord.

Father, help us to lay our disappointments with people at Your feet. People can let us down in such big ways. Some don't follow through with what they promise. Some are not the people we think they are, and we are left floundering trying to figure out what to believe is true. Some people take things we say or do the wrong way and we don't understand how people can look at the same things we do and yet walk away with such differing perspectives. We can have the best of intentions, yet there will always be someone that finds fault. Help us to let go of our hurts and disappointments and lay these things on Your altar, Father. These are some of the things we need Your help and Your peace to accept... The things we cannot control. Help us entrust them to You and let go, Lord.

Abba-Father, some days are just harder than others, but through it all You are faithful and we praise You for that, Lord. Thank You we can always count on You. Even if You don't do things in our timing, or You give us different answers than we expect, You haven't forgotten or forsaken us. For those who doubt that today, Lord, please, speak to their hearts in a way that will make them trust and believe You. Lord, please, speak Your truth into our hearts. Give us courage to keep putting one foot in front of the other and to keep going on the difficult days and on the good days, may we not take them for granted, but may we treasure them in our hearts.

Lord, this day and at this hour, we ask for Your Holy Spirit to speak healing and wholeness and peace to us. Let us breathe out the stress and cares and worries and pain and breathe in Your peace. May Your countenance shine down on us and give us rest from the long journey and give us the strength for what lies ahead.

May this day be laced with moments of laughter and moments of looking past the darkness and solitude that can take over our hearts and may we instead feel the warmth of Your presence coursing through us. Greater are You, Lord, Who is in us, than he who is in the world. Help us stand on that truth today. You are greater... You are our help... You are our refuge... You are our peace... And You are the lover of our souls. Thank You for this day, Lord. Please, be our shield and guide us this day. In Jesus' name we pray, Amen.

More Information

Debbie Kay is the founder of Hope For The Broken-Hearted Ministries and a ministry partner of Joni Eareckson Tada's ministry, Joni and Friends. She lives with her son, Ryan, in California and through the far-reaching power of technology and social media, she brings hope to millions of people around the world.

Through just her ministry on Facebook, she has reached over 10 million people per week with daily prayers, words of encouragement and resources that offer hope for the hurting, grieving and disabled. She has founded multiple support groups on Facebook where the number of members has reached 3,000 people in just a matter of months.

www.HopeForTheBrokenHearted.com, her website, is a haven for people searching for answers and resources pertaining to such topics as depression, grief, death/loss, divorce/relationships, chronic illness/disability, special needs children and much more. Her first hand experience with these subjects, in addition to her training and certification as a minister, grief recovery specialist and Life Coach (with specialties in Hope Coaching, Health and Wellness Coaching, Stress Management, Divorce Recovery and Marriage Mentoring) has made her a go-to source of information. She is constantly adding to the databases as she discovers helpful resources that might offer hope and healing.

On her website, she also offers an extensive database specific for teens which includes topics such as bullying, suicide and addictions.

BOOK BONUS: One of the highlights of Debbie's daily prayers are the beautiful scenic photographs that are posted along with the prayers. To make this paperback book reasonably priced, we were not able to include those pictures in this book. The e-book versions of "Prayers for the Broken-Hearted" do include the photos. Our free gift to those who have purchased this book is a complementary PDF version of "Prayers for the Broken-Hearted." Download your free copy at http://bit.ly/WNaD40.

CPSIA information can be obtained
at www.ICGtesting.com
Printed in the USA
BVHW090548301220
596440BV00008B/1067